AF322647

# UNLOCKING CREATIVITY

# UNLOCKING CREATIVITY

## *Artistic Inspiration Guide*

JULES HAWTHORNE

QuantumQuill Press

# CONTENTS

Copyright © 2024 by Jules Hawthorne

All rights reserved. No part of this book may be reproduced in any manner whatsoever without written permission except in the case of brief quotations embodied in critical articles and reviews.

First Printing, 2024

# CHAPTER 1

# Introduction

It has been put together in the order of the artistic process. There is no right or wrong way to be creative, but over the years, a pattern has been noticed in the way people have learned to be creative. The aim of this guide is to help individuals recognize what stage they are at in their creative process and to help guide them to the next stage, or to help unblock them if they are feeling stuck with a particular project. It is aimed towards people with an artistic flair, but as creativity can be applied to anything, this site may be helpful to musicians, students writing a thesis, etc.

This workbook study guide has been produced to aid an individual in unlocking his or her creativity. The writer believes that creativity starts with an idea and then blossoms into something all its own, an expression of who you are. Everyone is creative in their own way, whether it is creating a beautiful meal, a child's birthday cake, or a piece of poetry or artwork. The website is geared to help people find and nurture their creativity.

# Understanding Creativity

Embedded within these processes are a series of traits that are identifiable amongst creative individuals. Creative people will have expertise in a particular area, which will then contribute in a major way to the problem-solving processes. They will be risk-takers, willing to expose themselves to potential negative outcomes in order to try out new ideas. They will be independent, often working on tasks alone and in their own time. They will be intrinsically motivated by the task rather than any external or material rewards. They will have a tendency to be persistent with tasks, experience higher self-confidence, and be able to tolerate ambiguity and anxiety surrounding the problem. Other personality characteristics of creative people include curiosity, openness to one's internal experiences, a preference for complexity, and divergent thinking.

Creativity involves a series of processes. It begins with a problem that needs solving, a question that needs answering or a decision that needs to be made. This stage is called searching. There is a period of time in which the problem is considered, but it produces no true progress towards a solution. This is called incubation. Following this, there is a period of time in which the person is not thinking about the problem, but an idea suddenly emerges. This is called insight. The final stage of the process is called verification and can occur over a varied period of time. It is the process of confirming that an idea is valid and it often involves further problem solving to make the idea work.

# CHAPTER 3

# Exploring Different Art Forms

Another important reason to delve into another art form is that combining skills from one medium with another can produce fresh, quirky, and unique results. Multimedia is high in demand, and with the array of digital technology available, it is easier than ever to produce. For example, you are a painter, but you have been practicing creative writing, both independent from each other. Why not try writing a short story to accompany one of your paintings? Before you know it, you may have invented a new world for yourself or even something worth sharing with others. This can open doors to new opportunities to present and even sell your work.

We all have our favorite medium to express ourselves artistically. For writers, it may be words, and for musicians, it's notes. However, even within each medium, there are forms that create variance. An example of this would be poetry or prose for a writer and jazz or classical for a musician. Trying out a new medium or style may present the opportunity to bring a refreshing and invigorating change to your life or to the life of another. Imagine expressing an idea through the medium opposite of what you would usually use. It may especially interest you and create the capacity to learn a new skill or develop an existing one.

A multi-faceted artist has the ability to work within different artistic mediums, therefore capturing a wider audience and stimulating a new wave of creativity unto oneself.

# CHAPTER 4

# Finding Inspiration

Time may be a factor when finding inspiration. So if you happened to have blocked time out to paint and you feel that you wastefully have no ideas, don't give up. Try to relax and remember that making an actual attempt to paint is a progression in itself. This attempt may free up your mind and ideas might come. If they don't, an alternative activity might be best and a lesson learned on another day of your experience.

Inspiration may strike at any time, so be ready. Try keeping a small notebook to jot down ideas that may come to you and to take with you everywhere. Some find that a tape recorder works well for this purpose too. Although at times it may come to you during the middle of the night, it is not necessarily the best idea to jump out of bed and start painting. Chances are, you will be tired and the work will reflect this. Instead, jot down some quick notes to help remember your idea for later.

First and foremost, if you are trying to force yourself to an idea, you will not create. Rather, you will only become frustrated. The key to finding inspiration is to seek it like being on a quest. Throughout this quest, you should look to grow and learn from experience, as it is your experiences that will help form your true inspiration.

# CHAPTER 5

# Developing a Creative Mindset

One of the keys to consistently accessing one's creativity involves developing an educated understanding of the creative process. Often, people know very little about the nature of their creative processes. Many prolific artists and innovators have described having a clear understanding of the differences between associative thinking and a more focused, deliberate thinking strategy. In a general sense, associative thinking is when ideas seem to come together on their own, and deliberate thinking is when one uses a specific strategy to logically work through a problem. Although this is an oversimplified view of the process, it is a good starting point for developing an understanding of the nature of creativity. With some strategies, you can intentionally increase the probability of having creative insights and become more efficient at problem-solving with creative results.

# CHAPTER 6

# Overcoming Creative Blocks

Prompts, projects, and goals, Oh My!: Certain projects have a lot of creative freedom that can seem overwhelming. Often, narrowing down a specific goal for a piece can help to better understand what to do. Try setting a specific goal or solve a problem with a definitive and achievable answer. Sometimes all you need is a nudge in the right direction and you're off. If it doesn't work the first time, try again.

Are you experiencing a creative block or a mental barrier preventing the generation of new ideas or problem-solving solutions? Are you finding it difficult to develop creative ideas in your art? The infamous 'blank page syndrome' or "artist's block" is a serious issue for many artists. Often, the block is caused by stress, self-doubt, psychological problems, an unwillingness to be vulnerable and take risks, or from overthinking the work. There are many theories about the right and left brain in relation to the block, but the neuropsychology of the block is not well understood. Even less understood are ways to overcome these blocks. Here are some steps to help you break through your creative blocks and get the creative juices flowing again.

# CHAPTER 7

# Embracing Mistakes and Failure

It is important to understand that there is no right or wrong in art, and that making mistakes can often lead to entirely new and innovative ways of creating. Accept that mistakes will happen, and when they do, give yourself time to reflect on them and why they occurred. Think of it as problem-solving. Often, mistakes can be turned to your advantage. A slip of the paintbrush can lead to a new discovery and refined technique. An incorrectly mixed chord progression can lead you to an unexpected and original melody. Sometimes the best ideas and work come from an unplanned result. Failure to recognize this and clinging to the old and now incorrect idea can be a hindrance to your creative growth.

No one likes to be wrong, make mistakes, or fail. Many of us have grown up in a society that places much value on correctness, and failure is regarded as a very negative thing. Nevertheless, the real fact is, making mistakes and failing are both very valuable and necessary components of success. To make a mistake is to be presented with a learning opportunity, and every time we fail, we are given a chance to try again. It is a waste to not live fully simply out of fear of making mistakes or failing. The truth is, we will fail, and we will make mistakes. It is a natural and unavoidable part of the creative process. Embracing these concepts and learning to see mistakes and failures as opportunities is crucial for the artist.

"Stumbling is not falling."

# CHAPTER 8

# Nurturing Your Artistic Voice

Perhaps the simplest way to describe artistic voice is to use the analogy of the voice and language of a person. The artist's visual language is formed from a unique vocabulary of line, tone, color, and form that is used to express ideas and feelings. This is similar to the verbal language we use to express ourselves with words. Over time, the artist develops a specific way of working with the elements of their chosen medium, similar to how speech habits and inflections become a specific part of a person's verbal language. From this, it can be said that the visual language an artist uses is essentially a personality type that is the artistic equivalent of an individual. This artistic personality is what is recognized in the artist's work, like a signature, and is what defines the artist's uniqueness.

Your artistic voice, usually developed over time, is the essence of your creativity. It's a reflection of your inner world. With it, you communicate your experiences, thoughts, and emotions through your art. It affects the emotional content, type of expression, and therefore the themes of your work. Once you recognize a well-developed artistic voice, it gives you a stronger sense of direction and purpose. You recognize where you would like to take your art and how to do that. You step outside the mold of imitating others and dare to express your individuality.

# CHAPTER 9

# Balancing Structure and Freedom

Therefore, it is possible to outline a potential solution to the problem. That is, the artist must first create a framework where work can progress freely and with as little inhibition as possible. This work must then become a self-imposed task upon the later reflective self. By identifying this task of freedom with the second self encapsulated by the sentiment Schiller speaks of, the artist must then seek to allow his or her work to elapse into a regression towards the childlike self, all the while resulting in the later work being a task upon the self that produced it. Therefore, beginning a process of not destroying the two separate entities of work and self, but a unification of the two in a similar fashion to the cycle of production and task.

Friedrich Schiller defines this problem in the play "Wallenstein" by using the metaphor of a garden. This garden, representing the human psyche, is divided into two separate sections. The first is termed the naive, the unreflective childlike self. The second is the sentimental, where a cultivated adult looks back at the freedom of youth with nostalgia. It is the second self that Schiller believes the artist must seek to recapture, and it is the fusion of this second self with the first childlike self that is the better-known goal of integration of id with ego.

Balancing structure and freedom: The most creatively productive environment rests somewhere between chaos and order. The challenge is to define the right balance that facilitates structure while allowing for necessary freedom. Structure imposed too directly can easily stifle and inhibit the creative process, while too flexible an environment can also become a hindrance in that it is easier to procrastinate or become distracted.

# CHAPTER 10

# Harnessing the Power of Imagination

Technique: Write down a scenario or situation you may be dealing with currently and the expected result. Take time to relax and let go of the situation briefly. Now, re-imagine the scenario with a different outcome. What do the details of the new outcome contain? Is it now a more suitable situation for you? Using this technique can help you decipher between the end results you desire and can ignite more possibilities to reaching that desired outcome.

The power of imagination is an extremely important catalyst to look at life situations from a higher perspective. When we imagine, we use our creative minds to form new ideas from existing ones. This is an extremely important process in your everyday life as well as manifesting. You are constantly using your imagination to help make a decision on the outcomes of situations. Developing your imaginative skills can lead to new ways of presenting ideas and can open doors to new possibilities for change.

# CHAPTER 11

# Incorporating Personal Experiences

Throughout the course of any one life, painful tragedies will always befall a person or those one is close to. The death of a loved one, the contraction of a terminal illness, and the recent catastrophe of the September 11th attacks are all examples of tragedy of differing severities. How one decides to handle the emotional stress of these events is ultimately determined by their own self-satisfaction in their current life. By asking themselves the question of whether they are happy or unhappy with their lives, it defines a person's level of content. If someone is unhappy, they may reflect back on what events changed their attitudes towards life to a negative stance. By examining this turning point and how the happening occurred, they can use their emotions as a method to prevent similar events from reoccurring and always try to improve their current situation. This contrasts with someone who is content with their lives. They may fear another similar tragic event and end up avoiding risks, deterring them from success in any endeavor. However, if they also realize the events that lead to good fortune and the amount of time invested in between, they can prevent these emotions from dying down and converting to other unhappy events.

Experiencing tragedies can affect one's life in more than one way; however, the way it affects you is wholly your decision. You can let it affect you in a negative way and prevent you from helping others, take solace from the recollection of when you were fine and of your successes, let it be a tool for motivation, believing you have all this time to improve the world, or let it take you to the extreme where it is almost consuming and detracts from your ability to help others and feeling sorry for yourself.

# CHAPTER 12

# Experimenting with Different Techniques

There are so many different ways to approach art, and many different techniques to try out. Go to an art store and grab some different types of paper and other textures to work with. Find new ways to confine your lines and marks. Whether you are using a fine tip marker or a piece of charcoal, the way you make a line can have a huge effect on your drawing. Different methods for holding the pencil will produce a different quality of line. Try using a new medium. If you are a painter, try to develop a sculpture. If you are a drawer, try doing a painting. An animator might want to create a storyboard. Using a different medium can free you from your usual way of creating and allow you to explore new ideas. Experiment with using art to say things that words cannot. Try working with strong emotions, such as happiness, anger, or sadness. Try to use your art as an outlet for the emotion. Some people find it can be very therapeutic. Create an illustration that is an expression of a specific word. If the word is confusion, ask yourself how you can illustrate confusion. This sort of exercise can greatly increase your ability to communicate visually.

# CHAPTER 13

# Cultivating a Creative Environment

Minimalism is also conducive to creativity. When surroundings are disorderly or cluttered, the mind will often mirror the conglomeration of ideas, with none standing out or developing fully. Choosing a few pieces of art that one finds inspirational can be beneficial, as they often provoke thoughts and offer fresh perspective, which may lead to further creative thinking. This is a good alternative to the habitual behavior of seeking brain stimulation from the television. Viewing multiple storylines simultaneously is likely to cause confusion and does not aid focus. Although television is the chosen method of relaxation for many, it is an enemy to creative thinking, firstly because it is a passive activity, and secondly because much of its content is comprised of negative and emotive news items or dramas, which activate the emotions but are not conducive to the relaxed state necessary for creativity.

Creativity often stems from connections and ideas formulated in the unconscious. Therefore, engaging in activities which bring the unconscious to the fore, such as dream work and visualization, can be effective for problem-solving and idea generation. These activities should be carried out in a relaxed environment with no pressure to produce and followed up by a walk or some other form of letting the ideas incubate while the conscious mind is occupied.

Allowing for a relaxed and tranquil environment is critical for eudaimonia to spread its wings and contribute to creative living. Inspiration commands environment. The definition of inspiration is "Stimulation of the mind or emotions to a high level of feeling or activity." The word inspiration infers an imparting of truth or. In order for one to be open to truth and reality, and thus inspired, a relaxed and undisturbed environment is essential. Heidegger talks about this as a condition for "primordial cognition". Jung points to the fact that self-realization is dependent upon one's ability to reflect and access the unconscious. Because the unconscious mind is a storehouse of all knowledge and experience, one must be able to tap into it regularly.

# CHAPTER 14

# Seeking Feedback and Critique

Another strategy is to document the feedback, either written or recorded. This way, the artist can go back to the critique at a later date, after some time has passed from an emotional reaction to the feedback. A useful method for a written critique is to make a list of the comments. Next to this list, make a second list of intentions in the piece. These two lists can be compared and will reveal whether the artist was successful in the intended statement. If there are conflicting evaluations of two different aspects of a piece, it might signal a problem in the entry or clarity of the statement. This method is helpful for artists because critique is often more work for the brain than the making of art. By being systematic about critique, an artist can spend less overall time on the critique and more time making the changes to improve the piece. Remember to thank the source of critique, as sometimes it can be a lot of work to evaluate another's art.

Prepare yourself for the critique by keeping an open mind. You must suspend defensiveness and listen. This is maybe the most difficult part. Critique can sometimes be more effective when the artist is not present. This is because the audience sometimes is not comfortable being honest in fear of hurting the artist's feelings. However, the artist can also be missing useful feedback and sometimes misinterpret the message of the critique. If the source of critique is vague, do not hesitate to ask for specific answers. This is also very effective to do when showing at an exhibit. Ask questions to people viewing your work. Take note of their reactions to the art and ask what that reaction was. This could lead to some valuable information that the individual didn't think to address.

It is important to solicit critique and feedback from those who will help judge the effectiveness of your artistic statement. Often, an artist's intention does not necessarily match the perception by the audience. It is difficult for an artist to see or understand various perceptions when they are so involved in the conception of an idea. Public reaction is the artist's gauge for how effective their statement has been. Seeking critique can sometimes be a difficult task. Often, friends and family are not as honest as they should be for fear of hurting the individual's feelings. This can sometimes lead to ineffective critique. The best way to get effective and honest critique is to seek out individuals who will be unbiased and are knowledgeable in the field of the art form. Oftentimes, professional art organizations that hold juried exhibits will offer critique from the juror. Taking a class and exhibiting work is a good way to get feedback on a consistent basis.

# CHAPTER 15

# Collaborating with Other Artists

Involving other people in your work can also require some sacrifice in artistic autonomy. As the project will only be partially yours, this may be at the cost of some creative control. Understand that compromise will be necessary, but this is not necessarily a bad thing, as considering other points of view and ideas can result in a new way of thinking that can greatly benefit your work in the long run. This may lead to personal growth and skill development, and you may learn things from your collaborator that you can use in your solo projects.

Keep in mind that collaborating with other people can sometimes result in tension, and it is no different when it comes to involving yourself in a collaboration with another artist. The sharing of ideas, techniques, and workspaces can lead to frustration and disagreement, but with a good understanding and communication with your collaborator, it can be an experience that is beneficial for both artists involved. The key is to know and understand what you and your collaborator want out of the project. This can be achieved by each making a list of personal objectives, and then coming together to decide on the project's objectives. Regular consultation about these objectives can help ensure that the project remains on track and that both parties are satisfied with the direction in which it is heading.

# CHAPTER 16

# Exploring the Intersection of Art and Technology

This first section describes ways that technology may influence art. Modern technology allows for greater experimentation in art and more potential for a finished project to be interacted with. Digital art may be a cliché example in exploring the intersection of art and technology, but it provides one of the most expansive examples of how technology influences art. Digital art can sometimes be a simulation of other art forms, rendering its style and appearance with startling accuracy. This may bring into question "Why use digital rather than the real thing?". Looking at the simulation as a positive thing, it removes the limitations of the real-world counterpart and may allow for a new level of perfection. If all of the possible simulated styles are tools readily available within the same program, then they can be used together without waiting for previous layers of paint to dry or purchasing another of the same tool. This is something that is not logical in practice with real art media and if taken advantage of, could bring new possibilities to art. Simulation is only one area where digital art meets with technology. A more radical approach is the creation of the generative system. Art is often created through the assembling of a variety of puzzle pieces within the artist's mind; using technology to assemble these pieces in an intelligent manner and rendering the result can be an alternative method. This has been attempted with simple collage assembly and also more recently with paintings in the style of old masters. As the AI improves, an artist could potentially offload the creation of some art, having settings to constrain the form of AI choices to the criteria of a project. This could be a controversial topic for the future.

# CHAPTER 17

# Understanding Art History and Movements

Many times, new art techniques are actually mutations of previous techniques. Dabbling in the traditional Japanese watercolor painting technique, for example, is an adoption of an Eastern style that has been modified and used by Western artists throughout many different movements in art history. It is also simple to see how knowledge of art history can influence and inspire artistic design. If an illustrator is tasked with creating a fantasy-themed video game, knowing about the Pre-Raphaelite and late Victorian art that is often entailed in fantasy themes, and also the more recent fantasy art movement, he's going to have a rich sea of visual information to work from and also gain some insight into the nature of the genre.

Art movements have significantly changed over time. Understanding and having knowledge of these movements can provide a strong base for creating artwork and can also inspire a work of art. Inserting your own work into a certain art movement can provide a great sense of satisfaction and can also give a great jumping-off point for what direction to take a piece. Using a movement as a starting point and a basis for a piece can also be a great learning experience. If you try and work in a Cezannesque style, for example, you're going to learn a lot about the Impressionist movement and Cezanne himself before too long.

# CHAPTER 18

# Finding Inspiration in Nature

Nature surrounds us everywhere, and it is a powerful tool when applied to creating art. Next time you feel stuck and uninspired, apply these techniques to unlock the creative power that lies dormant in the world around you. It is a common misconception that nature-based art is largely painting landscapes and geode-inspired pottery. In actuality, any piece of art can be influenced by nature. Consumers of art often feel at peace with compositions that bring the outdoors inside. Stained glass work, still life paintings, and art photography can embody the peace and serenity that the outdoors provide us. Add nature to the inside of your daily environment and seek inspiration from its simplicity and order. Flowers, shells, and interesting pebbles are all usually interesting subjects that can be found cheaply or for free. Developing a bonsai tree is said to be a Zen-like hobby and can offer a wealth of inspiration. Much in the same way that a bonsai artist trims, wires, and shapes their tree, a ceramicist can apply those same techniques and ideas while sculpting in their chosen medium. Take a moment to jot down a list of things that you most enjoy doing outside. Hiking, bird watching, and journaling are all examples of applicable hobbies. The next time that you create art, try to capture the good feelings that you have from said activity. This helps to create a visual reminder of happy times and positivity and instills good work and patience habits with success just beyond the finish. Many artists find that smoking a bit of nature's greenery helps to relax the mind and let time pass, but only you know if that's right for you. Lastly, consider the fact that much of our planet's natural beauty is in danger or short-lived. You can consider creating activist art or joining a group or forum in search of camaraderie and inspiration.

# CHAPTER 19

# Exploring Cultural Influences

Cultural experiences often have been identified as a source of artistic inspiration. This exercise will guide you in considering how your culture has influenced your creative process. Take a moment and think about how you would describe your own culture. What music, foods, traditions, languages, and ways of interacting with people are common in your home environment? Now make a list of the most important influences that you can remember from your childhood to the present day. Consider family traditions, media influences, and any meaningful experiences with people from the same or different cultures. Now considering this list that you have made, reflect on your own patterns of creativity. How do you know when you are feeling inspired? Are there settings or activities where you tend to feel more imaginative? How do you generally capture ideas? Do you need to be alone or with others? Write spontaneously about your cultural influences and your patterns of creativity. How do these influences show up in your creative work? A specific example of a time when you felt very inspired and produced something original can be very useful in seeing a new connection between culture and creativity.

# CHAPTER 20

# Using Symbolism and Metaphors

Because the sequence of thoughts or feelings that make up any extended play or storyline are not subject to direct expression, the symbol is the principal means of rendering them into visual form. As with the metaphor, this often requires associative thinking: the establishment of visual images that are wordlessly related in a sequence corresponding to the sequence of thoughts or scenes that they are intended to represent. This type of symbolism might not always be obvious to the viewer, but that is of no consequence provided enough cues are given to allow the informed observer to interpret the symbolism correctly.

Symbols are a visual form of metaphor. Both function to provide a tangible means of expressing an intangible thought or feeling. But in the case of a symbol, the relation between the visual image and the abstract idea is fixed by usage and is not subject to interpretation; it is generally an agreed-upon conventional relation. For example, the cross is a symbol of Christianity, the red rose a symbol of social-ism. The complexity of painting allows a wider latitude for the use of symbols; for example, a contemporary Christian painting might depict Christ on the cross standing in a clear-cut forest, the cross and the tree both being used as symbols of death and rebirth.

# CHAPTER 21

# Exploring Color Theory and Composition

Reflection Activity: Make an artwork that aims to express specific concepts or emotions through the use of color. Once it is completed, write a short essay breaking down your usage of color, how key elements of color theory were utilized, and how successful you were in rendering your intended imagery. The artwork should be simple and nonrepresentational in nature to force awareness on color alone. (e.g. try a still life of a group of objects under an exotic light source, while focusing more on the way light affects the color of the objects as opposed to the objects themselves)

The first part of this chapter discusses the nature of color and is divided into stages of emotional response to color. It goes into more detailed color psychology and delves into the various schools of thought on the concepts. It finishes with the effects of color design and how different combinations can lead the eye or be a vehicle for contrast. Later, the chapter delves into the basics of color theory. It provides a comprehensive overview of color theory and how to incorporate it into works of art, acting as a jump point for artists who've never been exposed to those concepts and as a refresher to those who have. Special attention is given to 3D art, digital art, and traditional 2D media. The chapter finishes off with an interview with a Japanese illustrator who provides insight into his personal praxis when it comes to the use of color in his illustrations.

# CHAPTER 22

# Capturing Emotions and Expressions

It can be really difficult to capture emotions and expressions accurately, but these are the very elements which make a piece of art, and which make one piece of art different from another. The problem can be sorted into two different sections. Firstly, you have to understand the expression that you are trying to capture. A person's expression is the result of their feelings, mood, and goals at a particular point in time. If you can understand what the person was feeling at the time, then you will be able to portray that feeling through your art to anybody who sees it. A good understanding enables you to capture expressions when people are not posing for you. For example, if you wanted to draw a friend who is reading, you might wait until they are engrossed in something and then quickly sketch their expression from the side. This is often a good way to catch natural expressions because the person is unlikely to be thinking about the fact that they are having their expression drawn. Just make sure that they don't notice you doing it, or they might get paranoid! This kind of quick sketch is known as "drawing from life";

it has a lot of benefits, but due to the transient nature of expressions, it is still best used to practice for the second method of capturing expressions. The second method is to consciously alter the mood of a piece of art until it reflects the expression that you are trying to convey. When you know which emotion you are trying to draw, brainstorm for all of the artistic elements that could convey it. For example, for sadness, you might use dim lighting and dull color; for anger, you might use strong lines and rough textures. This method is excellent training for your manipulation of mood in a piece of art, but it very often results in an image that looks artificial and forced. The reason for this is that the elements of an image are not isolated; they combine to form a whole that is greater than the sum of its parts, and an emotion is a complex thing. In a real-world scenario, you might only want to convey one part of a complex emotion because it is part of a larger story. For example, a self-pitying person feeling sorry for themselves because they will not have to work, but he is still happy to be on holiday. This requires the understanding of the mood, so it is best to acquire the mood of a posing session for method two into method one.

# CHAPTER 23

# Pushing Boundaries and Taking Risks

Boundaries are the norms of society; when we work within these prescribed limits, creativity is stifled. Not all boundaries can or should be pushed, but in general, the process of stretching against and perhaps walking beyond them is essential to growth and change. Taking risks involves a willingness to fail. Artists who fear failure and its shameful relatives - ridicule and humiliation - may never step outside the lines, much less dance on them. They play it safe and in the long run, this is the riskiest of all. Without an ability to risk the self, which involves making a leap into the unknown, a leap that may end in dissolution of what we know as our self, but also a chance of reconstituting the self at a higher level, one is always stuck in the same place. No formula exists for pushing boundaries and taking risks, but all creative work involves a leap of faith into the unknown and a willingness to risk failure. This takes a certain degree of courage and a willingness to act in spite of fear. All acts of creation are also acts of destruction or transformation. When we create a painting, we destroy a blank canvas, when we create a child, we destroy our previous identity as non-parent and transform our lives forever. The creative process is a journey into the unknown, which necessarily involves giving up the known, the safe, the comfortable or familiar. It is a heroic journey which ultimately may lead to the boon of new self-knowledge and an expanded awareness. Taking risks and pushing boundaries ultimately is a means of confronting and overcoming obstacles, which results in personal growth and increased self-esteem, the opposite of failure.

# CHAPTER 24

# Balancing Realism and Abstraction

Price's painting, on the other hand, is highly abstracted in comparison but exhibits the same advantage of being able to understand what is going on. In this case, the abstracted method is successful and does not cause confusion. This is an important point because often a disadvantage of abstraction is a loss of clarity and a tendency towards ambiguity. This can alienate the viewer and cause communication breakdown because people tend to assume that all art is a language of signs and any art that does not seem linguistically translatable is deemed unreadable. This assumption is not always correct. Abstraction, in terms of breaking down images into their fundamentals, is still an effective communication tool for form. Many abstractionists aim to distill the essence of an object into a simple and pure form that carries the same information. This is a high-level artistic activity and a potent learning tool. The ability to manipulate form in this way can greatly teach an artist about the nature of form and the myriad ways it can be represented. This knowledge is highly transferable to realism, and an artist who understands it will be able to represent form and its transitions with confidence and a deep comprehension.

In discussing the feats and pitfalls of attaining such a synthesis, it is worth exploring what abstraction and realism bring to art. What are the advantages of abstraction or realism? According to symbolist painter Philip Amos, "true realism comes from abstraction," meaning that in order to represent form convincingly, the artist must interpret the visual data into a concrete formula. This is akin to an abstraction. The formula is the general and essential information that constitutes the object's form, and this can be more "real" than the form itself. This occurs frequently in painting, and in many mediums, an artist will often have to simplify complex visual information in order to make it readable. Clarity is a characteristic that is generally associated with realism, and it has a lot of power as a communicating tool. A concrete example of this is a painting by AD Greer where folds of a jacket are painted in a simplified manner, yet the way they turn the form is unmistakable.

In the past, we have discussed the spectrum between realism and abstraction. As schools of thought, they represent two extremes and, in practice, the vast majority of art is not purely one or the other. Sometimes art is called abstracted realism, other times realistic abstraction. In some cases, it is filled with seemingly unattainable balance.

# CHAPTER 25

# Creating Art with Intention and Purpose

Intending to paint a feeling is an especially efficient means to add depth to an artwork. Emotions are visualized by symbolism and color, making them a fine field for expression in painting. An artist wishing to do this needs to start by thinking about the feeling and what it is that evokes it. Then, he must decide on the right way to symbolize this in a painting. This will usually involve researching the feeling and the history behind it. The final result is the translation of what has been discovered into a visually accessible form. At the end of the process, there should be tangible evidence of the initial intent, and the viewer will be capable of realizing what the artist set out to do.

An artist inspired can see a profound effect on the general result of his endeavor. Yet, to generate art that is honestly fulfilling, it is vital to have intent and function. Without intent, a work of art can be thought of as mere exercises with no real end goal. Many present-day painters without a clear vision, throwing on colors until they create a fascinating form or composition. While there is nothing incorrect with this approach, it often lacks inspiration and depth. By having intent at the beginning of the artistic process and sticking with it throughout, an artist can effectively paint whatever he sets out to, adding a great deal to a piece's depth and coherency. Intent is the thought; the purposeful plan behind a work of art. This can range from wanting to capture an emotion, to translating a topic, to exploring a vision, or simply practicing a specified methodology to its completion.

# CHAPTER 26

# Exploring Different Artistic Mediums

Since the time of traditional and classical placements, more and more artists have put different styles and ideas into the fleeting context of the present day. Postmodernist thought is an abstract process that, in various mediums of art, seeks to depict the present state of society and to achieve the most direct interpretation of the world using strategies from a host of various traditional thoughts and applies them to handicrafts with a strong conceptual and purposeful intent. This idea of the future being a host of stylistic reinvention has caused it to be a difficult task to locate a universal medium of art. Many contemporary artists, realizing this, have returned to a pluralistic and open-ended concept of art where it can be anything. In doing so, one of the most accommodating is the medium. In the pluralistic state of contemporary art, almost any material may be used, and it opens the door for a plethora of styles and ideas. By experimenting with different mediums, it allows for the artist to fully realize their expressive capabilities. There are many different categories of mediums to explore, and most of them have not been used to their potential. It is an exciting time for artists, and the options are virtually unlimited.

# CHAPTER 27

# Developing a Personal Style

It is important that the student expose themselves to a variety of influences and not solely focus this exercise on one particular artist or painting, as this can become a subconscious form of plagiarism. Over time, with the influence of various other factors and influences, the student will use this knowledge in a mixed amalgamation of techniques that will produce a stylistic result of their own.

To develop a personal style, the student should copy masterworks. A masterwork is a painting that has had a profound influence on the development of art. By studying a masterwork and attempting to copy this painting stroke for stroke, color for color, the student will gain some understanding of the thought processes and techniques that the artist employed. Although it sounds tedious and sometimes disheartening when certain passages cannot be executed, it is an enormously helpful training and should be persisted with. The value of the exercise is not the finished product but the understanding gained from it. With this knowledge, the student will be able to employ some of these techniques in their own work and use what they have learned in future pictures.

# CHAPTER 28

# Exploring Artistic Techniques from Around the World

Mudcloth, also known as bogolan, is a type of fabric that is hand-woven and dyed using fermented mud and leaves. It is a traditional craft of the Bamana, who are an ethnic group in Mali. The process begins by weaving the plain cloth using a narrow strip loom. The cloth is then dyed with a yellow solution obtained by soaking the leaves of the n'gallama tree. It is then dried in the sun for 2-3 days, after which it is painted with designs using a piece of iron or wood that had been dipped in the fermented mud. The mud is from three specific mud pools, each with unique qualities. The darker mud comes from the pools furthest from the village and is the most durable. After the entire piece of cloth has been painted with the mud, it's then boiled in water and left to dry. This process creates a chemical reaction, turning the design from yellow to the eventual black it will wind up. The woven and dyed squares are then sewn together and used to make clothing or blankets. Though it is the most viable form of income in this area, the pressure of the modern world has heavily strained this tradition. It is said that there are now only 5 men who still know the ancient art of making bogolan. This has been seen as a factor in why these villages have been declared UNESCO World Heritage sites, to try and secure some funding for the men to pass on their knowledge to the next generation. Mud-cloth is currently influenced by the world, and many craftswomen are adding new intricacies and designs to their work that have never been seen prior. This is a controversial issue as this is beginning to warp the traditions and styles of an ancient artistic practice.

# CHAPTER 29

# Incorporating Music and Sound into Art

There is a very direct and immediate relationship between sound and art. The rhythmic aspect of the pulsation of sound clearly has its visual counterpart in light - this is not difficult to demonstrate. The nature of sound as a temporal art form presents a challenge when it comes to trying to represent it in visual terms. The essence of a powerful piece of music can be a potent source of inspiration for any artist. It is here that new ground can be broken, particularly if we try to understand the true personal effects of a piece of music and examine how this already influences our perception and daily lives. This area of study can yield fascinating results, particularly in the field of psychology, and it is an approach that has many contemporary applications in music and image re-mapping for advertising and propaganda, but these are other stories.

# CHAPTER 30

# Using Art as a Form of Self-Expression

Self-expression is easily the most important reason for creating art. It is what drives you to create art. You can use art as a means to express what you feel in a non-threatening and introspective manner. Let's face it, it's often easier to open up a box of crayons and create a picture than to sit down and talk about what is bothering you. It is more comfortable and less intrusive. Through creating art, you may be able to bring traumatic events to the forefront of your mind and deal with them in a more positive and controlled way. By bringing repressed feelings to the conscious mind, you are able to deal with them and eventually put them to rest. Art therapy is a fantastic way to learn more about yourself. By simply taking some time out of your day to create art, you can escape the troubles of everyday life and take a journey into your imagination. You may find that the day's stress and problems melt away as you are caught up in the creation of art. Try to make a habit of setting aside an hour or so each week to focus on creating art, simply for the sake of expression and self-exploration. Use this time to try different things and to document how you are feeling at that particular point in time. Over the coming weeks and months, you may wish to compare your work to see how both your art and your emotional state have changed and developed.

# CHAPTER 31

# Embracing the Unexpected in Art

One of the most exciting facets of art making is that things can take unexpected turns. At times, the medium will lead you to unanticipated results. When artists are open to change, to being flexible, they will be able to take advantage of the unexpected and incorporate it into their work. An artist may start a piece with one intent and have it transformed by an experience. An artist who is forever seeking the final definitive draft will have a hard time embracing change, risk, and the unexpected. Usually, it's fear that keeps one from taking risks and trying something new. Low-risk art is about playing it safe, doing what you know will work because it has already been done before. This can keep an artist stuck repeating the same forms, subject matter, colors, and concepts. Artists who embrace the unexpected in their work usually have a distinguishing trait known as originality.

# CHAPTER 32

# Conclusion

So it will often be said that a person has a good idea or hunch but doesn't know it. This fits in with our analysis because he cannot verbalize his feeling that he knows when he follows it. During these periods, it is important to sift and sort through the details of your environment and find out all that impinges upon you that is conscious. Those seeking the promotion of both personal and general welfare will find in these pages a guide for the more precise building and reconstruction of the factors that affect knowledge and opinion.

Finally, remember to revisit the Positive-Sensitivity Decision-Making Model to help lay down all expected patterns of goal-fulfillment. A greater understanding of what you can expect from your actions will help generate initial outcomes and employ feedback that will result in the artful life. But the Logical Positive-Sensitivity Decision-Making Model is for another day.

Examine your stream of consciousness in relation to the "rightness" of your actions and inactions. In the final analysis, some of the things you do will seem to make the greatest sense, and some of the things you just would have refrained from doing. There are many ways in which you can know about the nature and consequences of what you do, too many to detail here. It is based upon your findings in these matters that you will regard yourself as acting responsibly or irresponsibly.

The peak creative state comes when you forget about yourself, your self-esteem, and whether your image will be affected if you do this or that. Once you are willing to do that, you will learn to trust your general ideas and impulses. And you will act more and more on hunches you can afford to follow. You will become more courageous and also surprisingly skillful in finding ways to avoid issues and actions that would be harmful to you. The trend of what you do will begin to show tremendous divergence from what you could have predicted for yourself.

www.ingramcontent.com/pod-product-compliance
Lightning Source LLC
Chambersburg PA
CBHW020752150726

48196CB00023B/755